Billions of Balls

Beth Dvergsten Stevens

Historical Toys

Perfection Learning® CA

Dedication

For all children who love to play with balls. With special thanks to Jana B. and Jim G. for their expertise.

About the Author

Beth Stevens is a writer and former teacher. She currently writes stories and develops crafts and games for children's magazines. She also writes a weekly newspaper column for kids. Her first book, *Celebrate Christmas Around the World,* was a teacher's resource book.

Although she's no longer in the classroom, she still loves teaching and learning. She hopes her readers will discover something new and interesting every time they open one of her books! Beth lives in Waverly, Iowa, with her husband, three children, and their pets.

Inside Illustrations: Michael Aspengren and Amy Sharp
Photo Credits: PhotoDisc, Inc. and Art Today
Book Design: Deborah Lea Bell

For information, contact
Perfection Learning® Corporation,
1000 North Second Avenue,
P.O. Box 500, Logan, Iowa 51546-1099.
Phone: 1-800-831-4190 • Fax: 1-712-644-2392
Paperback ISBN 0-7891-2874-8
Cover Craft® ISBN 0-7807-7832-4

Table of Contents

Chapter 1. The History of Balls 5

Chapter 2. The History of Ball Games . . 12

Chapter 3. Let's Play Some Games! . . . 24

Chapter 4. Let's Make a Ball! 35

Chapter 5. Ball Trivia 41

Appendix Types of Balls 50

The History of Balls

You can throw it and catch it. You can roll it and kick it. You can bounce it, bat it, and "head" it. It's as old as dirt. What is this toy? It's a ball!

The ball is the oldest toy around. Every child has played with one. Children even played with balls in ancient times. Children of all ages have tossed and rolled balls.

Most early balls were about 2½ inches wide. That size fit a child's hands just right.

But today, not all balls are the same size or shape. There are different balls for different games. Balls are used in more games than any other toy.

Some balls are big. Others are tiny. Some are hard. Others are soft. Some balls can even bounce sky-high.

There are balls as light as air. And some balls are heavy enough to break your toes! Some balls are used with bats, clubs, or rackets.

There are balls with holes. And balls with dimples. Balls with stitching. And balls that are smooth. Each ball is made for a special purpose.

What was the very first ball? It might have been a rock! It might have been used as a weapon!

Perhaps a caveman picked up a rock.

Then he threw it at an animal. Maybe he missed.

The caveman wanted to be a good hunter. So he practiced. But soon he found out it was fun to practice!

His children tried it too. Soon they were playing games with the rocks.

In the British Museum, you can see a stone ball. It is 5,000 years old! This kind of ball was found in Scotland and Egypt.

Sometimes it was painted. This stone ball wouldn't be good for soccer or baseball! But children had fun rolling it to one another.

Not all balls were used for play. Some cultures believed balls brought good luck.

After people planted their crops, they did special things with balls. They played catch from east to west to bring sunshine. They dipped balls in the river to bring rain.

Were all ancient balls made of stone? No. Children made balls from things they found. If they lived where it snowed, they made snowballs!

If children lived near trees, they carved balls from the wood. Sometimes they even wove leaves into balls.

Children used other things too. They shaped balls from clay in their backyards. They played with round gourds that grew in their gardens. And they made linen balls from plants they grew.

Some families raised cows or sheep. Children made leather balls from cowhide. They made wool balls from sheep's fleece.

The children sewed the wool or skins together into a ball shape. Then they filled the ball with hair, grass, feathers, or seeds. Sometimes the balls were even filled with dirt!

Hundreds of years ago, European children learned to make bouncing balls. They used the bladders of sheep or goats. They filled them with air.

On tropical lands, children made a different kind of bouncing ball. They used the milky juice of special trees. This juice became stretchy as it dried.

The trees were rubber trees! When Columbus landed in the New World, he saw children playing with these rubber balls.

Today, balls are made of many different materials. Lots of balls are plastic. Wiffle® balls and beach balls are plastic. Some plastic balls even look like leather!

Balls like Ping-Pong® balls are made of thin celluloid. This is a thin plastic. The balls are very light.

Balls like Nerf® balls are foam. Playground balls and Superballs® are made from a rubberlike material.

Many balls are still made of leather. Leather balls cost more than plastic ones. They are used in college and professional sports.

Some new balls are like some of the oldest ones! One is the Hackey Sack®. It's just a small leather ball filled with pellets. Children played with this kind of ball thousands of years ago.

Yes, balls are very old toys. But people of all ages still play with them. And every time you play ball, you are repeating history!

Chapter 2

The History of Ball Games

Children and adults have always played games with balls. Some games use only a ball and the skill of the players. Some games need special equipment.

Games with Bats

Baseball is an American game. But it's like some old games played in England. People there played Rounders, Cricket, and Townball.

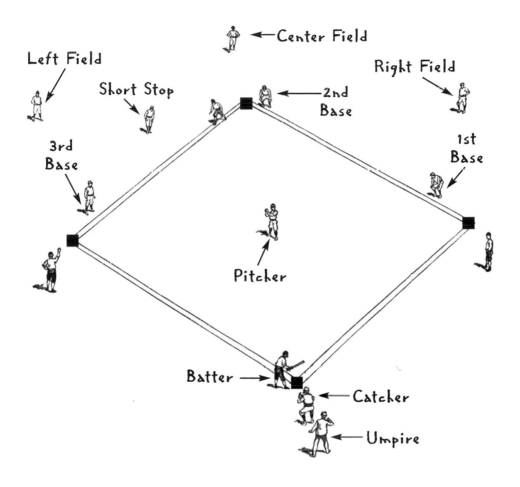

Left Field

Center Field

Right Field

Short Stop

2nd Base

3rd Base

1st Base

Pitcher

Batter

Catcher

Umpire

Today, each baseball team has nine players. They play on a field. It's shaped like a diamond. There are four bases. Teams take turns batting the ball.

If the ball is hit, the batter runs around the bases. To score, the batter must reach all four bases.

The other team fields the ball. If the batter doesn't reach a base, he's out. Three outs means the other team gets a turn at bat.

Softball is like baseball. Years ago, people wanted to play baseball inside. So they made some changes.

They made the ball bigger and softer. They put the bases closer together. And the bat became shorter.

Softball was a slower game. And it could be played in gyms or barns!

Today, people play fast-pitch and slow-pitch softball outside.

Wiffle® ball is like baseball. But the ball is different. It is made of white plastic. It's hollow and has many holes.

The Wiffle® ball was invented in the United States in 1953. A young boy wanted to play baseball in his backyard. His father didn't want any broken windows! So he invented the Wiffle® ball.

The plastic ball is light and safe. The holes help pitchers throw curve balls.

Games with Pins

Skittles started a very long time ago. It was played outside with heavy balls. In Germany and the Netherlands, the game was played inside.

Nine skittles, or pins, were set up in a diamond shape. Players rolled a wooden ball to knock them down.

Today we call this game bowling. But we use ten pins in a triangle. The ball is heavy and large. And it has three finger holes.

Games with Baskets

In 1894, basketball was invented in the United States. The first baskets were wooden peach baskets.

There were nine players on each team. Players tried to throw a ball into the basket. After every score, someone had to get the ball out of the basket! Now a rim and net are used.

Today's teams have five players. They shoot

the basketball in many exciting ways. Even
high school players try to dunk the ball!

Games with Nets

Volleyball started in 1895. It was played
inside. It was less tiring than basketball.
Women didn't play much
volleyball until 1926.

Now volleyball is
popular for people of all
ages. There are six
players on each team.
Players serve the ball over
a high net. They hit the ball
back and forth. The serving team scores
when the other team cannot hit the ball
back.

Games with Walls

Handball began in Ireland 1,000 years
ago. Today it is played on a court with walls.

Players wear special gloves. But a glove is worn only on one hand.

They hit a ball against the wall with their hand. The ball bounces all over. It can even bounce off the ceiling! Handball can be played by two or four players.

Games with Rackets or Paddles

About 800 years ago, tennis started in France. It is played on a court. The court can be grass, clay, blacktop, or concrete. There can be two or four players.

Players hit a bouncy felt ball back and forth across the net with rackets. The net is low to the ground. A player scores when the opponent misses a returned ball.

Lacrosse is the oldest game in North America. It became the national game of Canada.

Players carry, pass, or bat a rubber ball with a netted stick. Only the goalie can touch the ball with his or her hands. Players score when they kick or bat the ball into the goal.

Ping-Pong® is the common name for table tennis. Ping-Pong® balls are lightweight plastic. Players use wood and rubber paddles. They hit the ball back and forth on a table. The ball must bounce over a net. Two or four players can play.

Pickle-Ball® is played in many gym classes today. It's a very modern game. It was just invented in the 1970s!

The game is a lot like tennis. Four people can play on one court. Players use light paddles to hit a small plastic ball over a low net. Pickle-Ball® can be played indoors or out.

Another modern game is racquetball. It began in the 1950s. It is played like handball. Players use a short racket. The racket is attached to the player's wrist with a strap. Players hit a bouncy ball against the walls.

Games with Goals

Football started in early Greece and Rome. The Roman football game was used to train soldiers. Their games were very rough!

Americans started to play football in the 1800s. There were 25 players on each team! Now teams have 11 players.

The first footballs were leather. There was a sheep's bladder inside, filled with air or straw. Later, rubber was put inside the football.

Players today wear pads and helmets to prevent injury. Each team tries to take the ball across the goal line to score. They kick, carry,  pass, and throw the ball. It is still a rough game. Players are knocked down and tackled!

Soccer is the most popular team game in the world. It is often called football in Europe.

The game is played with a round ball. It is made of small pieces of leather. Players try to kick the ball into a netted goal.

Players cannot touch the ball with their hands. But they can bounce it off their chests, heads, or feet!

The goalie tries to keep the ball out of the goal. She can use her hands.

Rugby is like playing football and soccer together. A rugby ball looks like a fat football. Players run, pass, and kick the ball to each other. Players tackle one another. But they don't wear pads or helmets! A rugby game doesn't stop after each play like football. Play continues until a goal is scored like soccer.

Games with Clubs or Mallets

Golf was invented by a shepherd in Scotland. He hit small stones along the ground with his staff. The stones rolled into a rabbit hole.

Golf came to America in the 1800s. Today players walk or ride around large grassy courses. They use clubs to hit the ball into 9 or 18 different small holes. Golfers count the number of hits it takes to get the ball into each hole. Low scores are good scores.

Croquet started in France and England. Today it is played by American families in backyards. Wire hoops are set up in the grass. Players use wooden mallets to hit heavy, colored balls through the hoops.

Chapter 3

Let's Play Some Games!

Have you ever played football or anty over? These are old games.

Have you played Pickle-Ball® or Wiffle® ball? These ball games are quite new. Maybe you play them in gym class or with friends.

There is no limit to the ball games you can play! Try some of these.

Wiffle® Ball

Set Up

Lay out a diamond-shaped field with bases like baseball. The rules are like baseball rules.

Needs

- two teams with an equal number of players
- Wiffle® ball and bat

Object of the Game

Score more runs than the other team.

Play

This game is played like baseball. One player pitches. The rest of the players on that team field the ball.

The team at bat hits the ball and runs around the bases. A player is out if a fielder catches a fly ball, tags the base, or tags the runner with the ball.

After three outs, the teams trade places. One point is scored each time a runner reaches home plate.

Anty Over

Object of the Game

Capture all the members of the other team.

Needs

- two teams with the same number of players
- playground ball
- low building

Play

Players form two teams. Teams go to opposite sides of the building. Team 1 yells "Anty over" and tosses the ball over the roof. Team 2 tries to catch it. If they miss, it's their turn to throw the ball. If they catch it, they run around the building to "capture" Team 1.

Team 2 throws the ball at a player on Team 1. Players touched by the ball are captured. Players not touched are safe.

Team 2 then throws the ball over the roof. Play continues until all players on one team are captured.

Kick Ball

Set Up

Lay out a diamond-shaped field with bases like baseball. The rules are like baseball rules.

Needs

- two teams with an equal number of players
- rubber playground ball

Play

The pitcher rolls the ball toward the kicker at home plate. The kicker kicks it and runs to first base. The fielders try to get the runner out. There are four ways to put a runner out.

1. Catch the ball before it touches the ground.
2. Tag the runner with the ball.
3. Touch the base first.
4. Hit the runner with the ball.

After three outs, the teams trade places. Points are scored each time a runner reaches home plate.

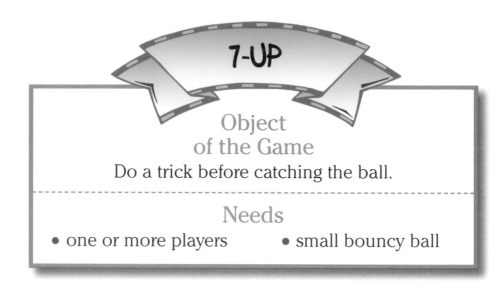

Object of the Game

Do a trick before catching the ball.

- -

Needs

- one or more players
- small bouncy ball

Play

Bounce a ball against a concrete wall. The player must do tricks before catching the ball. If player misses a trick, he or she starts all over.

Try these tricks or make up your own!

- **Ones**   Clap once. Do this once.

- **Twos**   Clap once in front and once behind your back. Do this twice.

- **Threes**   Toss ball under your leg and clap. Do this three times.

28

- **Fours**   Snap fingers. Do this four times. Add one more snap each time.

- **Fives**   Spin around. Do this five times.

- **Sixes**   Do a jumping jack. Do this six times.

- **Seven-up**   Stand with your back to the wall. Toss the ball over your shoulder. Then spin to catch it. Do this seven times.

Another trick you might try is slapping your legs. Or cross your hands over your chest and clap. Or you might toss the ball then clap under each leg. Try doing a toe-touch.

Four Square

Draw a large square on the concrete with chalk (about 8' x 8'). Divide it into four smaller equal squares. Label them A, B, C, and D. Draw a diagonal line across square A. This is the server's square.

Object of the Game
Bat the ball around the square without missing.

Play

One player stands in each square. The server bounces the ball one time and then bats it with her hand to another square. That player lets it bounce once and then hits it to another square. If a player misses, a new player takes that place. Or the player goes back to square D and other players move ahead one square.

Keep Away

Object of the Game
Get the ball away from the other two players.

- -

Needs
- 3 players
- any size ball

Play

Player 1 stands between two other players. These two toss the ball back and forth. Player 1 tries to take it away. If Player 1 gets the ball, the player who tossed the ball last is the new Player 1.

Circle Ball

Object of the Game

Be the only player left.

Needs

- many players
- any size ball

Play

Players stand in a circle. Players throw the ball to one another.

If a player drops it, he is out. Or she gets a letter of some word such as *pig* or *horse*. When a whole word is spelled out, the player is out of the game.

Circle Dodge Ball

Object of the Game

Be the only player left in the circle.

Needs

- two teams with an equal number of players
- rubber playground ball

Play

Team 1 stands in a large circle. The other team stands in the center. The players on Team 1 throw the ball at the players inside. Players inside move around to miss the ball. When a player is hit, he joins Team 1. The winner is the last player left in the circle. The teams trade places for the next game.

Chapter 4

Let's Make a Ball!

Long ago, kids couldn't buy balls at stores. They had to make their own. Now you can make some old-fashioned balls too!

Then use your new balls! Play a game of catch or a bouncing game. Make up a new game to play!

Cloth Balls

Some of the first balls were made from cloth or leather. They were filled with seeds, horsehair, or even dirt! Make this cloth ball with an old sock! It's good for throwing and catching games.

Needs
unpopped popcorn
measuring cup
3 plastic grocery bags
scissors
masking tape
old sock
needle and thread

Steps

1. Put ⅔ cup popcorn into a plastic bag. Hold it in your hand. If you want a bigger ball, add more popcorn. If you want a smaller one, take some out.

2. Put this bag of popcorn inside the other bags. You will have three layers of plastic. Hold the ball of popcorn. Twist the bags tightly above ball.

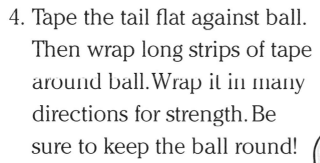

3. Cut off extra plastic. Leave a short tail.

4. Tape the tail flat against ball. Then wrap long strips of tape around ball. Wrap it in many directions for strength. Be sure to keep the ball round!

Step 5A

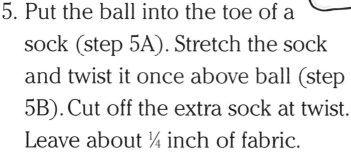

5. Put the ball into the toe of a sock (step 5A). Stretch the sock and twist it once above ball (step 5B). Cut off the extra sock at twist. Leave about ¼ inch of fabric.

Step 5B

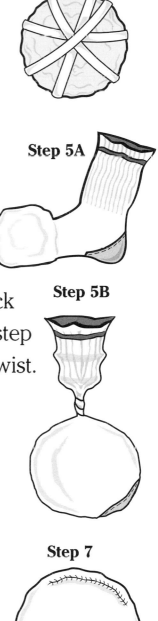

6. Sew a long running stitch around cut edge of sock. Pull thread tightly to gather edges together.

7. Sew the edges together with small stitches. Press the gathered edges flat as you sew. Knot the thread and cut.

Step 7

Felt Dodecahedron Ball

This ball has 12 sides!

These balls are more than 2,400 years old. Then they were made from 12 pieces of soft leather.

Each of the 12 pieces had five sides. The pieces were sewn together. Then the ball was filled with grass, straw, or hair.

You can make a ball from colored felt scraps. It won't be perfectly round. But it works well for many games.

Needs

12 different colors of felt

pentagon pattern

pencil

scissors

needle and thread

stuffing—polyester fiberfill, shredded foam, feathers, or dried beans

Steps

1. Trace around the pattern on the felt.

2. Cut out each piece.

3. Stitch the pieces together into a ball shape. Use a whipstitch. (You might want to ask an adult for help.)

4. Leave one side open. Fill with stuffing. Stitch the opening closed.

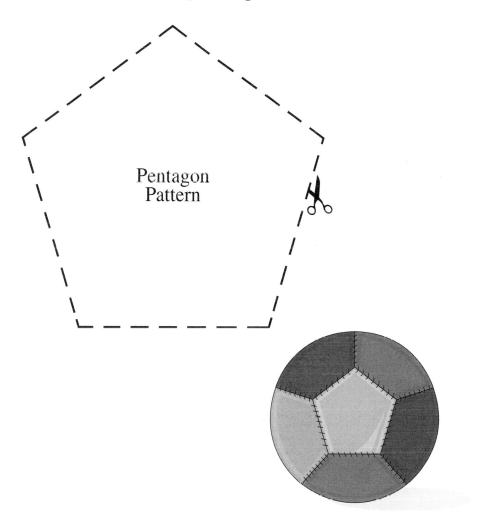

Pentagon
Pattern

Rubber Ball

Children made bouncing balls from the milky liquid from rubber trees. You can make a

Needs
50 wide rubber bands
old newspapers or cotton batting

simple rubber ball with rubber bands. It won't bounce as high as a Superball®, but it will work for lots of games!

Steps

1. Crumple newspaper or batting in your hand. Is it the right size for a ball?

2. Stretch the rubber bands tightly around the wad. Stretch them in all directions. Be sure your ball is round.

3. Use all the rubber bands. Try not to twist them. Be sure bands are smooth and as flat as possible on the last layers.

Chapter 5

Ball Trivia

Strange Ball Games from the Past

* That's one heavy ball!
  In the 1500s, Aztec Indians in Mexico
  played a game with a five-pound
  rubber ball! Players tried to keep the
  ball in the air.

  Then they bounced the ball through
  a stone ring on the wall. But they
  couldn't use their hands. They could
  only hit it with their elbows, hips, or
  knees! Ouch!

- You'd get a workout with this ancient game!

  Indians in Mexico formed two teams. Players took turns kicking a wood or stone ball. They kicked it for 30 miles or more! The first team that reached the finish line won!

- Piggyback Ball

  Long ago in Egypt, girls played catch with a very light ball. It was made of papyrus fibers or flax. If a girl missed her catch, she carried another girl piggyback until that girl also missed! Try it sometime!

papyrus—a spiky plant that grows in the Nile River. The stems were used to make paper, sandals, mats, and ropes.

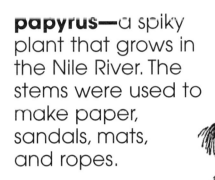

flax—a plant with blue flowers. The strong fibers are spun into yarns and woven into a fabric called linen.

- **Don't try this on your street!**
  In Ireland, people played a game called "road bowling." The ball was made of iron. It weighed two pounds. Players bowled the ball along the road. The player who reached the finish line with the fewest throws won. Maybe the streets in Ireland didn't have much traffic then.

- **Look, Mom. No Hands!**
  In Malaysia, there is a game that is played over a net. It is played much like volleyball. But the ball is small and light. And players cannot hit the ball with their hands! They must use other parts of their bodies. Try this game with a wad of crumpled paper or a Nerf® ball!

Balls, Balls, Balls

- Early Japanese balls were made of tissue paper. They were wrapped tightly with lots of string.

- In South America, children put seeds or pebbles inside balls. They rattled!

- In Africa, some balls were threaded with colorful beads.

- On islands in the West Pacific Ocean, children made balls from coconut leaves. In Samoa, they used palm tree leaves. These balls were square!

- A factory in Connecticut makes 100 Wiffle® balls every minute!

- In baseball, some pitchers throw fastballs more than 100 miles per hour!

- An inflated basketball should bounce 49 to 54 inches when dropped from 6 feet.

- Softballs have 88 stitches. Count them!

- The first baseballs were wound by hand. People put a walnut, bullet, or rubber ball in the center. They wound yarn or strips of rubber around it. The leather cover was sometimes made from old shoes!

- Pickle-Ball® was named after a dog who liked to chase balls. His name was "Pickles."

- Who puts the black stripes on a basketball? Factory workers do. They paint each stripe by hand. In one day, a worker can paint 800 balls! A really fast painter can paint 1,000!

- How did golf balls get dimples? A man in Scotland made a golf ball. It was rubbery. He tried the ball. It didn't go very far at first. But the more he hit it, the farther it flew.

  Then he looked closely at the ball. It had dents! Every time he hit the ball, it dented. But it went farther each time. The dents helped the ball stay in the air.

  Today, factories put 336 dimples in each ball. Dimpled balls fly four times farther than smooth balls!

- Balls for official games must be perfect. They are usually made of leather or rubber, not plastic.

Look inside a baseball

Outside Layer—The cover is thin cowhide. It is sewn on by hand with red cotton thread. There are 108 stitches! A factory worker can sew four balls in one hour. - - - - - - ->

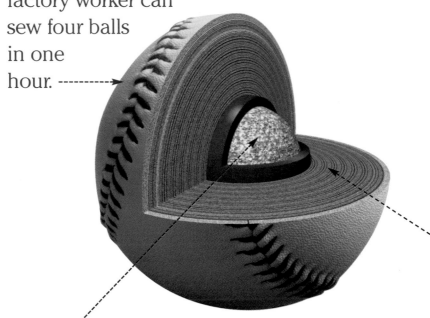

Inside Layer—The <u>core</u> is made from cork and covered by black and red rubber.

Middle Layer—The core is wrapped with 300 yards of wool yarn. It is usually blue-gray in color. Then a layer of white yarn is wrapped around the ball. And then another layer of blue-gray yarn. Last, a thin layer of cotton yarn is wound around everything.

Appendix: Types of Balls

Take a closer look at these balls. Which ones have you played with?

Type	Size
Basketball	• 30" around • about 20–22 ounces
Soccer Ball	• 27"–28" around (Youth balls are smaller.) • 14–18 ounces
Volleyball	• 25"–27" around • 9–10 ounces

Type	Size
Bowling Ball	• 27" around or less • 16 pounds or less
Rugby Ball	• about 11" long and 24"–25½" around the middle • 13½–15 ounces
Football	• about 11" long and about 21" around the middle • 14–15 ounces

Type	Size
Lacrosse Ball	• about 7⅞" around • about 5 ounces
Tennis Ball	• about 7⅞" around • about 2 ounces
Racquetball	• about 7" around • 1.4 ounces
Handball	• about 1⅞" in diameter • about 2.3 ounces

Type	Size
Softball	• about 12" around • 6–6¾ ounces
Croquet Ball	• about 10" around • about 16 ounces (one pound!)
Baseball	• about 9" around • about 5 ounces
Wiffle® Ball	• about 9" around • about ½ ounce

Type	Size
Golf Ball	• 1.68" • 1.62 ounces or less
Ping-Pong®or Table Tennis Ball	• about 4¾" around • ¹⁄₁₀ ounce

Think About It

Question

How many baseballs are used during a pro game?

Answer

As many as 50 baseballs might be used in one game today!

Some just get dirty. Others are foul balls hit into the crowd. The lucky fan in the crowd usually keeps the ball!

Question

Why did Egyptians put balls into ancient tombs?

Answer

For fun! Egyptians believed the dead could still play with their favorite toys.

Question

What was a ding-dong ball?

Answer

A baseball with a bell inside! The bell helped the umpire make the right call.

Question

Why do baseballs have seams?

Answer

So that pitchers can throw curve balls, knuckleballs, and sliders. Seamless balls won't fly through the air like that.